Ready or Not

(Here I come)…

Ryan Ball

SRL Publishing

www.srlpublishing.co.uk

#BreakingTheSilence

SRL Publishing Ltd
42 Braziers Quay
Bishop's Stortford
Herts, CM23 3YW

First published worldwide by SRL Publishing in 2020

ISBN: 978-0-995732391

READY...

written and
illustrated by

Ryan Ball.

I remember all of the noises,

They'd start quiet, but then they'd grow.

There was SMASHING...

...and CRYING...

But that was

a long time ago.

Now it was gonna

be different,

I had weapons and

ammo inside,

I had to be sure

And brave

And strong

And I'd need my

hat on outside.

I've read all about this in a book before,

So I know just what to do,

You can't go over, under, or around,

Oh, no, I'd have to go through!

It's always quiet in the forest

At least that's what I thought!

Ssshhh!

(Like a mouse)

I think it's
got me now!!!

HEY...?!

How...?

Again!

How are you?

I miss you.

Whats it like there?

because purple is your favorite color.

Today I learned to ride my bike

Again!

I've got you...

With the *important* things again.

I'd better head back home to carry on

He's okay.

I'm sick to the back teeth of this game,

I tediously trudged after him

All the time

Growing more and more bored.

AAARRRGGHHH!!!

At least that's what I thought

It's always quiet in the forest

I've got no time for myself at the moment,

There always seems stuff to do,

But I know if you want to set things straight,

There are hoops that you have to jump through.

And strong

And I'd need my axe for outside!

I had to be confident

And brave

The time was right to make a change,

I was ready for a bumpy ride,

But that was a long time ago.

...and *SCREAMING*...

...and *CRYING*...

It was all the echoes of noises,

Of every type you could know.

There was *SMASHING*...

NOT....

written and
illustrated by

Ryan Ball.